Germany

by Shirley W. Gray

Content Adviser: Professor Sherry L. Field,
Department of Social Science Education, College of Education,
The University of Georgia

Reading Adviser: Dr. Linda D. Labbo,
Department of Reading Education, College of Education,
The University of Georgia

COMPASS POINT BOOKS

Minneapolis, Minnesota

Compass Point Books
3722 West 50th Street, #115
Minneapolis, MN 55410

Visit Compass Point Books on the Internet at *www.compasspointbooks.com* or e-mail your request to *custserv@compasspointbooks.com*.

Cover: Neuschwanstein Castle in Bavaria, Germany

Photographs ©: Photri-Microstock, cover, 8, 12, 27, 29; Photo Network/Paul Thompson, 4; Photo Network/Chad Ehlers, 5, 6, 9, 33, 41; Spencer Swanger/Tom Stack and Associates, 10; Photophile/ Bachmann, 11, 43; Photri-Microstock/Kulik, 13, 30; Photri-Microstock/Bachmann, 14; Unicorn Stock Photos/Margo Moss, 15; Telegraph Colour Library/FPG International, 16; Fritz Polking/ Visuals Unlimited, 17; Warren Stone/Visuals Unlimited, 18; Photo Network/Phyllis Picardi, 19; Hulton Getty/Archive Photos, 20, 22, 28, 38, 39; Unicorn Stock Photos/Chuck Schmeiser, 21; David Brauchli/ Hulton Getty/Archive Photos, 23; Bachmann/ The Image Finders, 24; TRIP, 25; Beryl Goldberg, 26; Photo Network/Esbin-Anderson, 32; TRIP/TH-Foto Webung, 34; Gary Milburn/Tom Stack and Associates, 35; Unicorn Stock Photos/ Jean Higgins, 36; McCutcheon/Visuals Unlimited, 37; TRIP/M. Barlow, 40; Photri-Microstock/ Mehlig, 42; Norman Owen Tomalin/Bruce Coleman, Inc., 44.

Editors: E. Russell Primm, Emily J. Dolbear, and Neal Durando
Photo Researcher: Svetlana Zhurkina
Photo Selector: Catherine Neitge
Designer: Bradfordesign, Inc.

Library of Congress Cataloging-in-Publication Data
Gray, Shirley W.
    Germany / by Shirley W. Gray.
        p. cm. — (First reports)
    Includes bibliographical references and index.
    ISBN 0-7565-0128-8 (lib. bdg.)
    1. Germany—Juvenile literature. 2. Germany—Social life and customs—Juvenile literature.
    [1. Germany.] I. Title. II. Series.
    DD17 .G7 2001
    943—dc21   2001001456

Table of Contents

▲ *A girl wears the traditional dress of Germany's Black Forest.*

Guten Tag!

"Guten Tag!" might be the greeting you hear if you visit Germany. This is how Germans say "good day."

Many people begin their visit in the city of Berlin. It is Germany's capital and largest city. Germany's full name is the Federal Republic of Germany. Germans call their country *Deutschland*.

▲ *Tourists walk through Berlin's famous Brandenburg Gate.*

Germany is a large country in Europe. The borders of Germany touch nine countries and two seas.

Germany is a little smaller than the state of Montana. It covers 137,796 square miles (356,892 square kilometers). Germany is divided into sixteen states, called *Länder*.

◀ *A family works in a vineyard in the German state of Baden-Württemberg.*

▲ Map of Germany

The Land of Germany

German children ski, fish, and hike in the mountains, rivers, and flat lands of Germany. Flat lands are also called plains. The plains of Germany stretch along the coasts of the Baltic and North Seas.

▲ *A skier races down a course.*

▲ *Ships in the busy harbor in Hamburg*

Ships and boats dock at seaports on these coasts. One of these seaports is Hamburg. It is one of the busiest ports in Europe. Every day, fishers sail out to sea from this port. They catch herring, cod, and many other fish.

▲ *Germany has rich farmland.*

Germany also has good farmland. Its farmers grow wheat, potatoes, and fruit. They grow enough food for everyone in Germany. They also sell food to other countries.

Several important rivers flow through central and southern Germany. People use these rivers to travel and to ship goods.

One of Germany's major rivers is the Rhine. Factories send their goods down the Rhine River to the seaport. Pollution is a problem because so many factories stand on the banks of the Rhine.

▲ *Gutenfels Fortress overlooks Pfalz Castle on the Rhine River.*

Bavaria is a large state in southern Germany. The city of Munich is the capital of Bavaria.

A big mountain range called the Alps begins in Bavaria. The Alps stretch all the way into Austria,

▲ *The Alps stretch from Germany through several countries.*

▲ *The Zugspitze in the Alps is the highest mountain in Germany.*

Switzerland, Italy, and France. People from all over the world visit the Alps. They hike in the summer and ski in the winter.

The Black Forest

▲ *Trees surround Hohenschwangan Castle in Bavaria.*

Years ago, forests grew everywhere in Germany. Then people cut down many trees to get wood and to clear land for farming.

In southern Germany, forests still cover much of

the land. One area in this part of Germany is called the Black Forest. The dark fir trees that grow there give the Black Forest its name.

Beech, birch, and oak trees also grow in the Black Forest. Birds, deer, red foxes, and hares are plentiful there.

▲ *The Black Forest is in southern Germany.*

Acid rain is hurting the trees in the Black Forest. **Smog** from the many cars and factories blows into the forest. Rain then washes the smog onto the trees.

▲ *New laws will help cut back the smog from German industry.*

▲ *Ferns grow beneath the forest's trees.*

Scientists are worried about the old forest.
Germany has passed new laws to keep smog out of
the air. This will help the trees in the Black Forest to
recover.

Divided Germany

Today's Germany was once part of an **empire**. A ruler named Charlemagne was the **emperor**. After he died in A.D. 814, the empire was divided into many small countries.

Kings and dukes ruled these countries. They often fought one another. The kings and dukes built castles with thick, tall walls to protect them. Many of these castles still stand in southern Germany.

▲ *The ruins of an ancient Roman bath in Trier*

▲ *Tourists enter the castle gate at the medieval town of Rothenburg.*

In 1871, Prince Otto von Bismarck made the small countries into one large country. It was called Germany.

For many years, Germany grew stronger. But its leaders wanted more power. This led to World War I (1914–1918). Germany lost this war.

▲ *Otto von Bismarck*

In 1933, Adolph Hitler became the leader of Germany. He started World War II (1939–1945). Hitler was responsible for the deaths of millions of European Jews and others.

▲ *American soldiers killed fighting the Germans in World War II are buried at the Durnbach cemetery.*

After World War II, Germany was divided into two countries—West Germany and East Germany. In West Germany, the people **elected** their leaders. The workers had good jobs and plenty of food.

In East Germany, the people could not choose their leaders. The people were poor and had hard lives.

Many East Germans went to live in the West. So East Germany built a wall through Berlin in 1961. Soldiers guarded the wall. They even shot people who tried to climb over it.

▲ West and East German soldiers patrol opposite sides of the Berlin Wall in 1964.

One night in 1989, many East Germans gathered at the Berlin Wall. They wanted East Germany to join with West Germany.

The people began to smash the wall. The soldiers did not stop them. By morning, the people had torn huge holes in the wall.

◄ *A man pounds away on the Berlin Wall as East German guards look on in 1989.*

▲ *A woman shops for flowers in the united Berlin.*

The next year, East and West Germany became one country again. The rest of the wall was torn down. If you visit Berlin, you can see bricks from the Berlin Wall in a museum. A line is painted on the streets where the wall used to stand.

Modern Germany

German factories are famous for their fine work. Their products are sold around the world. People in the United States can buy German cars, tools, and watches. Munich is famous for computers and other high-tech products.

▲ *BMW cars are built on assembly lines that use robots.*

The leader of the German government is the chancellor. All Germans over the age of eighteen vote to elect the chancellor. Germany is now a **democracy**.

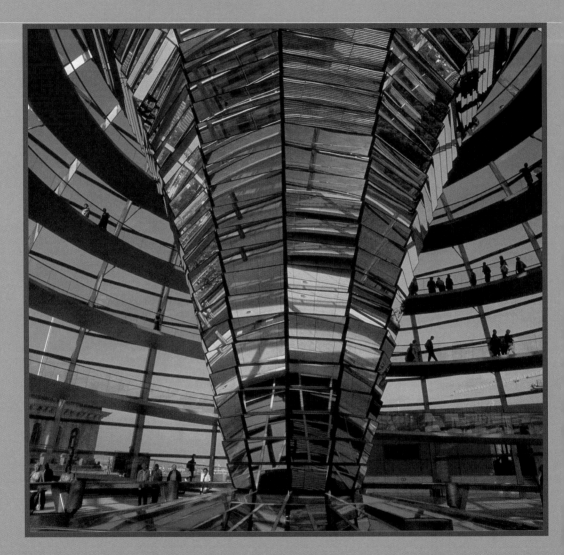

▲ *Mirrored dome atop the Reichstag, Germany's government building, in Berlin*

▲ *The Cologne Cathedral glows in the night.*

Germans are free to choose their religion. Most people are Christian. They belong to the Roman Catholic or Protestant Churches.

Before World War II, many Jewish people lived in Germany. But, during that war, millions of European Jews were murdered by the Germans. Some escaped to live in other countries. Few Jews live in Germany today.

▲ Children were photographed in 1945 after they were released from the Ravensbruck concentration camp.

Large highways cross the landscape of modern Germany. They are called *autobahns*. There is no speed limit on autobahns. The highways are very busy most of the time.

Cars on the autobahns pollute the air and water. The smog that they make causes some of Germany's acid rain.

▲ *Germany's autobahns have no speed limits.*

▲ *Children hike to a Bavarian lake.*

Family Life

In some ways, families in Germany are like families in the United States or Canada. Children go to school while their parents work. All children start school when they are six years old. They have to attend school until they are about fifteen years old.

After school, many German children eat fast food and watch movies. They also listen to music and play computer games.

Young people in Germany like to play football. In Germany, however, "football" is the game people in North America call soccer! Germany has thousands of local soccer clubs.

On weekends, German families like to spend time outdoors. Most families also vacation together in the summer. They usually take a month of vacation. Many Germans enjoy visiting other countries.

Families like to go hiking, ride bikes, and have picnics. On a picnic, they might eat *wurst*, a kind of sausage, on a roll.

▲ *Biking is popular in Germany.*

Festivals and Celebrations

▲ *People fill the streets of Munich during Oktoberfest.*

Towns and cities all over Germany have **festivals**. The largest festival—Oktoberfest—is held in Munich.

Oktoberfest started in 1810. That year, Prince Ludwig invited people to celebrate his wedding. The

▲ *A mother and her children decorate Christmas cookies.*

party was so much fun that it has gone on every year since! Oktoberfest lasts for sixteen days in late September and early October.

On the night of December 5, many German children hope for a visit from Saint Nicholas. According to an old story, Saint Nicholas puts candy and coins into the children's shoes. When the children wake up on Saint Nicholas Day, they find these gifts. Weeks later, many Germans celebrate Christmas by decorating trees, giving gifts, and going to church.

◄ *Carnival time in Cologne*

Cities near the Rhine River celebrate Carnival in the winter. They have parades, street fairs, and costume parties.

Carnival usually begins in February and ends on Shrove Tuesday. Shrove Tuesday is the day before the beginning of the Christian season of Lent.

▲ *Cuckoo clocks for sale in the Black Forest*

People around the world enjoy music, food, and other things created in Germany. Did you know that cuckoo clocks are made by people who live in southern Germany?

Johann Sebastian Bach and Ludwig van Beethoven are two famous German **composers**. Bach played the organ and many other instruments. So did his brother, his father, and his grandfather. He also learned how to write music. You might hear some of his music at a symphony concert, a wedding, or even on television.

◀ *A statue of Johann Sebastian Bach stands in Liepzig, where he wrote many of his famous works.*

Ludwig van Beethoven was born in Germany. He moved to Austria when he was a young man. He studied Bach's music and then began to write his own.

Beethoven got sick while he lived in Austria. He lost his hearing. Yet, he continued to write beautiful music, even though he could not hear it!

▲ *Ludwig van Beethoven*

▲ *Jacob and Wilhelm Grimm*

Do you know the story of Snow White and the seven dwarfs? Do you know the story of Cinderella and her magic pumpkin? These stories are part of a collection of folktales known as *Grimm's Fairy Tales.*

Two brothers, Jacob and Wilhelm Grimm, collected these folktales and some 200 other stories. They traveled through the German countryside in the early 1800s. They wrote down stories that people shared with them.

Some people think Germany's greatest gifts to the world have been food and drink. Sausages, chocolate, beer, and wines made in Germany are sold all over the world.

Have you ever eaten a piece of Black Forest cake? It is a delicious mixture of cherries, chocolate, and whipped cream. Of course, it is named after Germany's famous forest!

▲ *German sausages are world famous.*

▲ *German beer is popular around the globe.*

Visiting Germany

Many visitors come to Germany each year. Some people visit the castles built along the Rhine River. Others hike in the Black Forest or ski in the Alps.

Visitors can also travel through the countryside just like the Grimm brothers did. The story "Hansel and Gretel" was first told near the city of Kassel.

▲ *Many people visit Heidelberg, a famous university city.*

▲ *Performers wear traditional costumes of the Rhine region.*

If you visit Germany, you will learn more about this wonderful country and its people. When you leave you might say, *"Auf Wiedersehen! Danke!* Good-bye! Thank you! I enjoyed my visit to Germany."

Glossary

acid rain—rain polluted by smog and acid

composers—people who write music

democracy—a country in which leaders are chosen by election

elect—to choose someone by voting

emperor—the male ruler of an empire

empire—a kingdom

festivals—celebrations

smog—a fog made heavier and darker by smoke and chemicals

Did You Know?

- The Rhine is the longest river in Germany. It stretches 542 miles (872 kilometers) through the country.

- There are 1,230 different kinds of bread in Germany.

- Just as you dial 9-1-1 in the United States for emergencies, people in Germany dial 1–1–0, or 1–1–2 for the fire department.

At a Glance

Official name: Federal Republic of Germany

Capital: Berlin

Official language: German

National song: Third stanza of "Deutschland-Lied" ("Song of Germany")

Area: 137,796 square miles (356,892 square kilometers)

Highest point: Zugspitze, 9,721 feet (2,965 meters)

Lowest point: Sea level at the coast

Population: 81,700,000 (2000 estimate)

Head of government: Federal chancellor

Money: Deutschemark (to be replaced by the euro in 2002)

Important Dates

1000 B.C. Tribes from northern Europe arrive in what is now Germany.

A.D. 800 Charlemagne's empire begins.

1618–1648 Germany fights in the Thirty Years' War.

1871 Germany defeats France in the Franco-Prussian War. The German Empire is founded.

1918 Germany is defeated in World War I.

1933 Adolf Hitler begins to create his Nazi government.

1945 Germany and the Nazi government are defeated in World War II.

1949 East and West Germany divide.

1961 The Berlin Wall is built.

1989 The Berlin Wall is opened up.

1990 Germany is unified.

Want to Know More?

At the Library

Littlefield, Holly. *Colors of Germany*. Minneapolis: Carolrhoda Books, 1997.

Peters, Sonja. *A Family from Germany*. Austin, Tex.: Raintree/Steck-Vaughn, 1998.

Pluckrose, Henry Arthur. *Germany*. Danbury, Conn.: Franklin Watts, 1998.

Venezia, Mike. *Johann Sebastian Bach*. Danbury, Conn.: Children's Press, 1998.

On the Web

German Recipes
http://soar.berkeley.edu/recipes/ethnic/german/indexall.html
For recipes for all kinds of German specialties

The German Way
http://www.german-way.com/german/
For information about the people and culture of Germany

Through the Mail

The German Information Center
871 United Nations Plaza
New York, NY 10017
To get information about Germany

On the Road

Goethe-Institut/German Cultural Center
1014 Fifth Avenue
New York, NY 10028
212/439-8700
To learn more about German artists, writers, and musicians

About the Author

Shirley W. Gray received her bachelor's degree in education from the University of Mississippi and her master's degree in technical writing from the University of Arkansas. She teaches writing and works as a scientific writer and editor. Shirley W. Gray lives with her husband and two sons in Little Rock, Arkansas.